Dirt Track Racing

by Ed Youngblood

Consultant:
Hugh Fleming
Director, AMA Sports
American Motorcyclist Association

Capstone Press
Mankato, Minnesota

Capstone Books are published by Capstone Press
151 Good Counsel Drive, P.O. Box 669, Mankato, Minnesota 56002
http://www.capstone-press.com

Library of Congress Cataloging-in-Publication Data
Youngblood, Ed.
    Dirt track racing/by Ed Youngblood.
    p. cm.—(Motorcycles)
    Includes bibliographical references and index.
    Summary: Presents the history of dirt track racing as well as information about
the equipment used, skills required, and safety measures involved.
    ISBN 0-7368-0474-9
    1. Speedway motorcycle racing—Juvenile literature. [1. Motorcycle racing.]
I. Title. II. Series.
GV1060.145.Y68 2000
796.75—dc21   99-053162

Editorial Credits
Angela Kaelberer, editor; Timothy Halldin, cover designer and illustrator;
    Heidi Schoof and Jodi Theisen, photo researchers

Photo Credits
American Motorcyclist Association, 9, 28, 43
Archive Photos/Crady Von Pawlak, 12; Archive Photos, 14
Flat Trak Fotos, cover, 7, 11, 22, 25, 26, 30, 33, 35, 36, 44
Harley-Davidson Motor Company, 4, 46
Motorcycle Hall of Fame Museum, 16, 19
Unicorn Stock Photos/Paul Murphy, 21

1 2 3 4 5 6 05 04 03 02 01 00

Table of Contents

CHAPTER 1

Dirt Track Racing

Dirt track motorcycle racers compete on outdoor dirt racetracks. These oval tracks range from one-half mile to 1 mile (.8 to 1.6 kilometers) in length. Most races include 20 to 25 laps around the track. Some people call dirt track racing "flattrack racing" because the tracks do not have banked turns. These turns are built up higher than the rest of the track.

Dirt track racers travel at speeds of more than 100 miles (160 kilometers) per hour. Some dirt track racers have reached speeds of more than 140 miles (225 kilometers) per hour.

American Motorcyclist Association

The American Motorcyclist Association (AMA) governs dirt track racing. In 1924, this

Dirt track racers compete on outdoor racetracks.

organization began to organize motorcycle races. Today, the AMA sanctions most motorcycle races in North America. Sanctioned races are official AMA racing events. These events follow AMA rules and guidelines.

The AMA sanctions both amateur and professional races. Amateur racers often have little or no racing experience. They do not race for prize money. Professional racers have more experience. They can earn money for racing.

Racing Classes

Today, AMA professional dirt track racing has three classes. These classes are the Grand National Championship Series, the Harley-Davidson Sportster Performance Series, and the SuperTrapp SuperTrackers.

The Harley-Davidson Sportster Performance Series and SuperTrapp SuperTrackers classes both use street motorcycle engines. These engines are installed in motorcycles that are sold at motorcycle dealerships. These engines also are called stock engines.

Grand National Championship motorcycles have two-cylinder engines. The cylinder is

Racers in the Harley-Davidson Sportster Performance Series ride 883cc Harley-Davidson Sportsters.

the space inside an engine where fuel is burned to create power. Two-cylinder engines usually are larger and more powerful than one-cylinder engines.

Grand National Championship motorcycles have 750-cubic centimeter (cc) engines. This measurement is the size of a motorcycle's engine. Harley-Davidson makes most of the engines used in Grand National Championship racing. Honda also makes some Grand National engines. Grand National Championship motorcycles are fast, powerful, and expensive. Only about 100 Grand National Championship motorcycles exist in North America.

Racers ride only 883cc Harley-Davidson Sportsters in the Harley-Davidson Sportster Performance Series class. The Harley-Davidson 883 has a two-cylinder stock engine. Harley-Davidson makes thousands of these engines each year. They are cheaper and more readily available than 750cc Grand National Championship engines. But they are not as fast or powerful.

The newest professional dirt track racing class is SuperTrapp SuperTrackers. SuperTrackers have 1000cc stock engines in dirt track motorcycle frames. SuperTracker engines have two cylinders.

Many motorcycle manufacturers make SuperTracker engines. These include Honda, Suzuki, Yamaha, Harley-Davidson, and Ducati. These motorcycles are as fast as Grand

SuperTrackers have 1000cc stock engines.

National Championship motorcycles. They also are less expensive to own and repair.

Sponsors

Companies sponsor two of the dirt track classes. These companies provide money to pay for the costs of holding races. They may also provide prize money for the race winners. Motorcycle manufacturer Harley-Davidson sponsors the Sportster Performance Series. Exhaust manufacturer SuperTrapp sponsors the SuperTrackers class. This company makes parts that allow waste gases to escape from motorcycle engines.

Many motorcycle equipment manufacturers also sponsor their own teams of racers. These companies provide racers with equipment and pay for racing fees. In return, racers wear the sponsors' logos on their clothing and equipment. Racers also may promote the sponsors' products in TV and magazine advertisements.

Many motorcycle equipment manufacturers sponsor their own teams of racers.

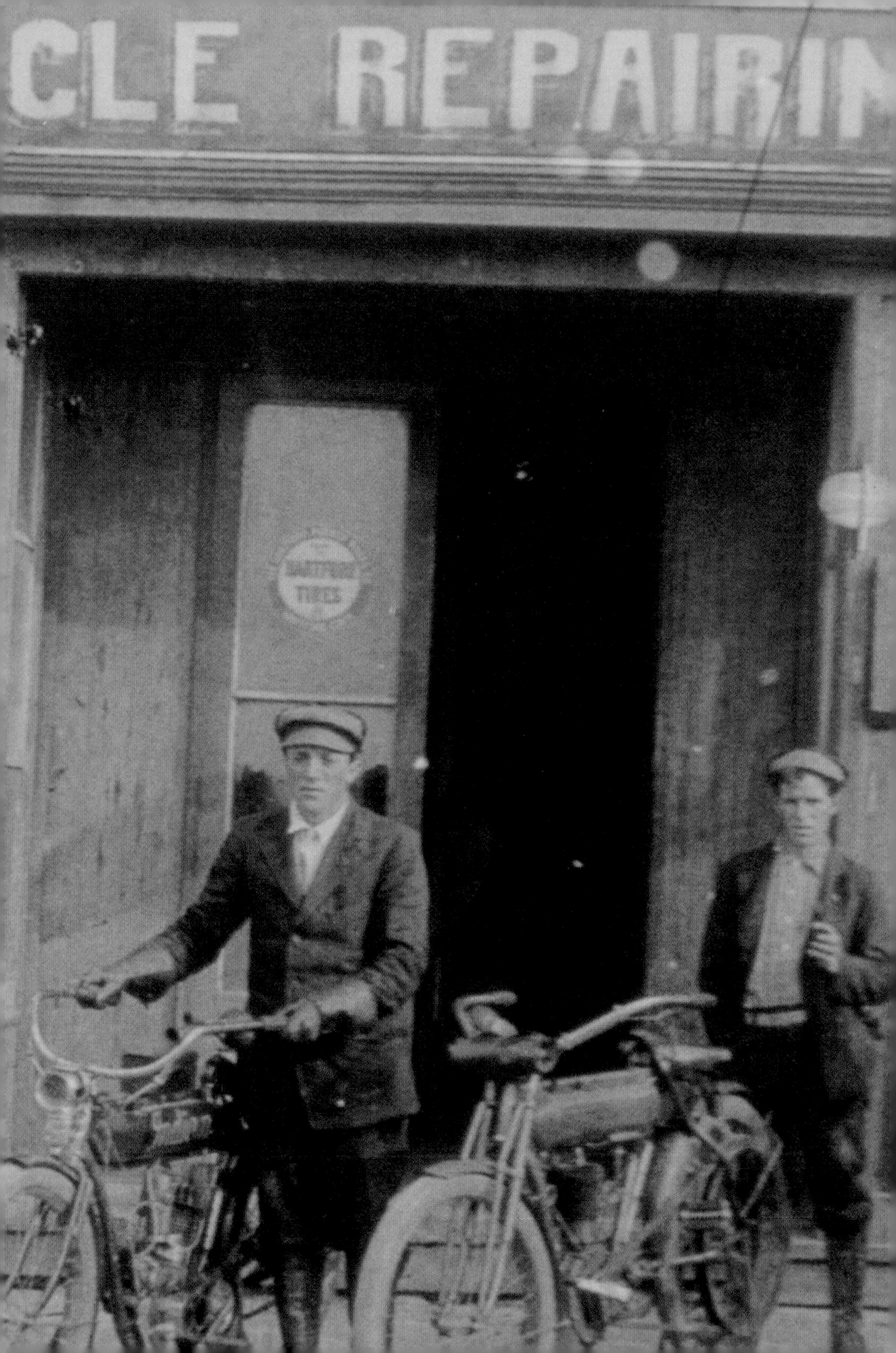
CLE REPAIRIN
HARTFORD TIRES

CHAPTER 2

History

Dirt track racing is one of the oldest types of motorcycle racing in North America. It began in the early 1900s.

Early Motorcycles
People first attempted to build motorcycles in Europe and North America in the late 1800s. They attached steam-powered engines to bicycles. These motorcycles were not very safe. Riders often sat directly above the engine. The engine's steam could burn the rider.

In 1876, German inventor Nikolaus Otto invented the internal combustion engine. This engine burns fuel inside the engine. In 1885,

The first motorcycles were built in the late 1800s.

Indian Motorcycle Company was a top motorcycle manufacturer in the early 1900s.

German engineer Gottlieb Daimler designed a motorcycle with an internal combustion engine. This engine was safer and more efficient than steam-powered engines. By 1900, many companies in Europe and North America were building motorcycles with internal combustion engines.

Before 1920, about 200 North American companies built motorcycles. These included

Thor, Excelsior, Cyclone, Indian, Flying Merkel, and Harley-Davidson. Of these, only Harley-Davidson still is in business.

Beginnings of Motorcycle Racing

In the early 1900s, motorcycle manufacturers wanted a way to test their motorcycles. Each company wanted to prove that its motorcycle was the best. About 1906, these manufacturers organized races to test their motorcycles and interest people in buying them. These were the first motorcycle races in North America.

Motorcycle manufacturers produced special motorcycles for racing. The first type of motorcycle racing was called Class A racing. Class A motorcycles reached speeds of more than 100 miles (160 kilometers) per hour. These motorcycles were designed to withstand races as long as 300 miles (483 kilometers). Class A motorcycles were too expensive for most people to buy.

The first Class A races were held at county fairgrounds. Most fairgrounds had an oval dirt track. These tracks were built for horse racing. But they also worked well for motorcycle

Dirt track racing's popularity increased during the 1930s.

racing. Each year, hundreds of Class A races took place throughout the United States and Canada.

Motordrome Racing

In 1908, some motorcycle racers raced on a different type of track. This type of track was built for bicycle races. These tracks were called velodromes because early bicycles were known as velocipedes. People later called these tracks motordromes when motorcyclists began racing motorcycles on them. The tracks were made of wood. They had steep, banked corners. This made them look something like oval bowls.

The shape of the motordromes allowed racers to reach high speeds. In 1912, racer Lee Humiston raced at a speed of more than 100 miles (160 kilometers) per hour at a California motordrome. These speeds led to many accidents and injuries. The tracks also were difficult to maintain. Races would often have to stop so workers could repair damaged tracks. This was expensive for track owners. These problems caused motordrome races to end in the mid-1920s.

Growth of Dirt Track Racing

In 1934, the AMA introduced Class C races. These races used standard street motorcycles. People could buy these motorcycles at motorcycle dealerships. This allowed more people to participate in motorcycle races.

The AMA also introduced other new forms of motorcycle racing. These included short track, tourist trophy, and road racing. Short track races take place on courses less than 2,000 feet (610 meters) long. Tourist trophy races take place on curving courses with jumps. Road races take place on paved racetracks. All of these forms of racing still exist today.

From 1946 to 1953, the AMA held one championship race at the end of each racing season. This 25-mile (40-kilometer) race was called the Springfield Mile. It took place at the Illinois State Fairgrounds in Springfield. The winner of the Springfield Mile became that year's national champion.

In 1954, the AMA changed this system. It held an annual series of 18 races called the Grand National Championship Series. The top 18 racers in each race earned points. This series included both dirt track and road racing events. The racer with the most points at the end of the racing season became the Grand National champion.

The number of points racers receive has changed over the years. Today, racers receive 23 points for first place, 19 for second, and 16 for

From 1946 to 1953, the winner of the Springfield Mile race became the dirt track national champion.

third. The next 15 racers receive from 15 points to 1 point.

In 1976, the AMA created separate classes for dirt track and road racing events. These classes still exist today.

Motocross Racing

In the 1980s, many young motorcycle racers switched from dirt track to motocross racing. Motocross races take place on outdoor dirt tracks that range from 1 to 3 miles (1.6 to 4.8 kilometers) in length. These tracks have obstacles such as hills, jumps, and sharp turns.

Racers had several reasons for switching to motocross racing. Motocross racers use serial production racing motorcycles. These motorcycles are cheaper and more readily available than AMA Grand National Championship class motorcycles. Grand National Championship class motorcycles must be custom built. These motorcycles are built one at a time. Each one may have different features. This makes them much more expensive than motocross cycles.

Dirt track motorcycles also use more expensive tires and fuel than motocross cycles. Dirt track motorcycles use special soft tires that give them better traction to grip the road. These tires usually wear out after one race. Dirt track motorcycles also use fuel that has a higher level of oxygen than standard gasoline. This fuel costs about four times as much as standard gasoline.

Many dirt track racers were concerned about the high costs of the sport. The AMA responded by creating two new dirt track racing classes. In

In the 1980s, many dirt track racers switched to motocross racing.

1993, the AMA created the Harley-Davidson 883cc National Dirt Track Series. In 1998, the AMA changed the name of this class to the Harley-Davidson Sportster Performance Series. In 1999, the AMA created the SuperTrapp SuperTrackers class. Both of these classes use street motorcycles. The AMA hopes these classes will create a new interest in dirt track racing.

CHAPTER 3

Equipment

Motorcycles are dirt track racers' most important pieces of equipment. But racers also need other equipment such as helmets and special clothing.

Parts and Controls

A dirt track motorcycle has controls similar to those of a street motorcycle. The racer's right hand operates the throttle. This device controls the motorcycle's speed. It serves the same purpose as a car's gas pedal. The racer's left hand presses the clutch. This lever allows the rider to shift gears. Racers shift gears to travel faster or slower. Racers operate the gearshift

A dirt track motorcycle has controls similar to those of a street motorcycle.

with their left foot. They operate the brake with their right foot.

All dirt track racing motorcycles have mufflers. These devices reduce the noise made by the engine. Dirt track motorcycle mufflers are less efficient at reducing noise than street motorcycle mufflers are. Dirt track engines are about 20 decibels louder than street motorcycle engines. Sound is measured in decibels.

All dirt track racing motorcycles have some parts removed. They have no lights, turn indicators, windshields, or fenders. These parts are not necessary for dirt track racing. Motorcycles are lighter and run faster without them.

Helmets and Clothing

Racers' helmets are their most important piece of safety equipment. A helmet protects a racer's head from injury during a fall or crash. Dirt track racers wear full-coverage helmets. These helmets cover the entire face and jaw.

Racers' helmets are their most important piece of safety equipment.

Dirt track racers' clothing also is designed to protect them from injuries. Racers wear padded leather suits. These suits protect racers' skin when they fall. The suits have additional padding at the shoulders, elbows, hips, and knees. Some racers wear a flexible plastic back protector under their suit.

All racers wear leather gloves and heavy boots. The left boot has a steel plate covering the bottom of the sole. Racers often use their left foot to help them slide through turns. This steel plate helps racers control their motorcycles when they slide sideways into a turn.

A racer's clothes are designed for safety. But they also help racing fans identify racers as they speed around the track. Each suit is brightly colored and custom-made. No two suits are alike.

Racers often use their left foot to help them slide through turns.

Scott Parker

Date of Birth: November 21, 1961
Hometown: Swartz Creek, Michigan
Turned Professional: 1979
First Victory: Du Quoin Mile race in Illinois
Honors: 1979 Dirt Track Rookie of the Year; Grand National champion in 1998, 1997, 1996, 1995, 1994, 1991, 1990, 1989, and 1988

Parker received his Grand National license in 1979 at age 17. At the time, he was the youngest racer ever to earn this license.

From 1979 to 1999, Parker competed in 366 races. He finished in the top 10 in 320 of these races and won 93 of them. Parker is a nine-time Grand National champion. He has won this title more times than any other dirt track racer.

CHAPTER 4

Skills and Safety

Dirt track racers must be highly skilled motorcyclists. They use strength, reflexes, and mental strategy in order to win. Most racers develop these skills through years of competition.

Licensing

Most racers begin their racing career at an early age. The AMA sponsors races for racers who are younger than 16. These young motorcyclists learn to race on small motorcycles. These motorcycles often are as small as 50cc. At age 16, racers who do well in amateur races can obtain a professional license. This document allows

Most dirt track racers develop their skills through years of competition.

dirt track racers to compete in AMA Grand National races.

As racers gain experience, they can receive licenses to race larger and faster motorcycles. Racers with two years of amateur experience can apply for a Pro Sport license. These racers may race 250cc, 650cc, or 883cc motorcycles. Pro Sport racers need 80 or more racing points per year to qualify for a Pro Expert license. These racers may race 250cc, 600cc, 883cc, or 750cc motorcycles. Pro Expert racers then can apply for a Grand National Championship license. Racers need 100 or more points per year for this license. Racers with a Grand National Championship license can compete in all dirt track racing events.

Most professional racers are men. But several women racers have earned an AMA professional dirt track license.

Racing Skills

Racers use strategy as they race. They try to be the first to make the first turn and enter the

Most racers begin their racing careers at a young age.

groove. This narrow strip of dirt often is near the inside of the track. Motorcycles travel faster on the groove. They also slide less and are easier to control. Grooves usually are so narrow that it is difficult for one racer to pass another. The first racer who enters the groove has an advantage over the other racers.

Racers use several moves to stay in control. As they turn, they slide sideways with their left foot on the ground.

Racers tuck in to decrease the air resistance around them as they race. To tuck in, racers bring their knees and elbows in as close to the motorcycle as possible. They lay forward on the gas tank and put their head down low.

Racers need good reflexes. They must react instantly to other racers' actions or officials' signals. This helps them stay safe as they race.

Safety

Safety is important in all types of racing. This is especially true of motorcycle racing. Motorcycle racers are not protected by an automobile body. Dirt track racers ride very close together. They also travel at high speeds.

Race officials help keep races safe. Many of the rules they enforce are designed to make races safer. Starters control the racing action. These people turn on a green light at the starting line. This signals the start of a race. During a race, starters and other officials also

Racers tuck in to decrease air resistance.

use colored flags to warn the racers. Officials may wave a yellow flag. This signals racers to slow down and be careful. A red flag signals racers to stop immediately. This may be because of an unsafe track or a serious crash.

Dirt track racers race very close together around the track. This sometimes makes it difficult for race officials to determine the winner. Officials often use a video camera to

J. R. Schnabel is one of the youngest Grand National dirt track racers.

record the race and determine the winner. This is called a photo finish.

Top Racers

Many of the top dirt track racers are from North America. Many racing fans believe the greatest racer ever is Scott Parker of Swartz Creek, Michigan.

Parker became a professional racer in 1979. From 1979 to 1999, Parker competed in 366 races. He finished in the top 10 in 320 of these races. Parker won 93 AMA Grand National Championship races. No other racer has won even half as many AMA Grand National Championship races. Parker became the Grand National champion nine times in the 1980s and 1990s.

Steve Morehead is one of the most experienced dirt track racers on the AMA national circuit. He was born in 1955 and began his professional racing career in 1972. He has competed in more than 340 races. He finished in the top 10 in nearly 70 percent of these races.

Chris Carr also has had a long racing career. He began racing professionally in 1985 and received the Rookie of the Year award that year. Each year, the AMA gives this award to the best first-year racer. In 1999, Carr became the Grand National champion.

J. R. Schnabel is one of the youngest Grand National dirt track racers. Schnabel was born in 1979. This was the same year that Scott Parker received his AMA professional racing license. In 1996, Schnabel became a professional racer. At the time, he was 16 years old. Schnabel did so well that the AMA named him the 1996 Rookie of the Year. In May 1999, Schnabel won the first SuperTrackers race. This race took place in Hagerstown, Maryland. Steve Morehead finished second to Schnabel in this race.

Dirt track racers' careers often last for more than 20 years. Racers often become friends as well as competitors. Racers help and learn from each other. They help new racers develop their racing skills. They want to make sure that dirt track racing will be a safe and popular sport in the future.

Grand National Champions

1999	Chris Carr
1998	Scott Parker
1997	Scott Parker
1996	Scott Parker
1995	Scott Parker
1994	Scott Parker
1993	Ricky Graham
1992	Chris Carr
1991	Scott Parker
1990	Scott Parker
1989	Scott Parker
1988	Scott Parker
1987	Bubba Shobert
1986	Bubba Shobert
1985	Bubba Shobert
1984	Ricky Graham
1983	Randy Goss
1982	Ricky Graham
1981	Mike Kidd
1980	Randy Goss
1979	Steve Eklund

Words to Know

amateur (AM-uh-chur)—a racer who does not earn money for racing

clutch (KLUHCH)—a lever that allows the rider to shift gears

cubic centimeter (KYOO-bik SENT-uh-mee-tur)—a unit that measures the size of a motorcycle engine; this unit is abbreviated "cc."

cylinder (SIL-uhn-dur)—the space inside an engine where fuel is burned

groove (GROOV)—the fastest path around the racetrack

internal combustion engine (in-TUR-nuhl kuhm-BUSS-chuhn EN-juhn)—an engine that burns fuel inside the engine

license (LYE-suhnss)—a document that gives official permission to do something

professional (pruh-FESH-uh-nuhl)—a racer who can earn money for racing

rookie (RUK-ee)—a first-year professional motorcycle racer

sanction (SANGK-shuhn)—to officially approve a race; AMA-sanctioned races must follow AMA rules and guidelines.

throttle (THROT-uhl)—a device that controls a vehicle's speed; a motorcycle throttle operates like a car's gas pedal.

velodrome (VEE-luh-drome)—a wooden track used for bicycle racing

To Learn More

Dregni, Michael. *Motorcycle Racing.*
MotorSports. Mankato, Minn.: Capstone
Books, 1994.

Jay, Jackson. *Motorcycles.* Rollin'. Mankato,
Minn.: Capstone Books, 1996.

Otfinoski, Steven. *Wild on Wheels:
Motorcycles Then and Now.* Here We Go!
New York: Marshall Cavendish, 1998.

Savage, Jeff. *Motocross Cycles.* Rollin'.
Mankato, Minn.: Capstone Books, 1996.

Useful Addresses

American Motorcyclist Association
13515 Yarmouth Drive
Pickerington, OH 43147

Canadian Motorcycle Association
P.O. Box 448
Hamilton, ON L8L 1J4
Canada

Cycle News
P.O. Box 5084
Costa Mesa, CA 92626-5084

Internet Sites

American Motorcyclist Association
http://www.ama-cycle.org

Canadian Motorcycle Association
http://www.canmocycle.ca

Cycle News
http://www.cyclenews.com

FlattrackNews.com
http://www.flattracknews.com

Index